There is Life After...

Linda H. Williams

There is Life AFTER...

Presented By:
Linda H. Williams

Foreword By:
Dr. Jo Anne White

"Inspiring Christian Authors to BE Authors"

Pearly Gates Publishing, LLC, Houston, Texas

There is Life After…

There is Life After…

Copyright © 2018
Linda H. Williams

Cover Design by Tia Jones

All Rights Reserved.
No portion of this publication may be reproduced, store in any electronic system, or transmitted in any form or by any means (electronic, mechanical, photocopy, recording, or otherwise) without written permission from the publisher. Brief quotations may be used in literary reviews.

ISBN 13: 978-0-991537-71-6

Some names and identifying details have been changed to protect the privacy of individuals.

Scripture references marked KJV, NIV, and NKJV are used with permission from Zondervan via Biblegateway.com.

For information and bulk ordering, contact:
Pearly Gates Publishing, LLC
Angela Edwards, CEO
P.O. Box 62287
Houston, TX 77205
BestSeller@PearlyGatesPublishing.com

What Others Are Saying

"What kind of relationships do you want with yourself and others? Option A: Healthy, happy, fulfilling relationships **OR** *Option B: Taxing, stressful, draining relationships? Option A, you say? Good. Read this book—twice. Buy a copy for each "Option B" relationship you have."*

~ Soul Dancer, Private Spiritual Teacher, Coach, Keynote Speaker, Syndicated Columnist, Founder of Soul University, and Executive Producer for Pay Radio ~

****

"Linda Williams is the epitome of what it means for one to pursue a quality life after tragedies that typically tend to cripple and misdirect so many. She is absolutely the proper author of this book and the message of hope and triumph it delivers."

~ J. Stokely, Founder/CEO of Royal Apex Kreations ~

****

"An awesome blessing to many as they read and are inspired by our Lord and Savior, Jesus Christ."

~ Joyce Bray ~

****

"Linda Williams' compilation of testimonies on "Life After" is rooted in scripture, as Proverbs 24:16 (NKJV) teaches us: "For a righteous man may fall seven times and rise again…" *These pages are filled with brave and transparent words of wisdom that will surely inspire and motivate you to have the best that God intended for your life!"*

~ Anita Price Lane ~

There is Life After...

"Author Linda Williams, a phenomenal woman with a wealth of knowledge and courage, has opened the door to peace. The powerful messages in There is Life After... *give us all a sense of peace, knowing we're not alone when life throws a curve ball. I highly recommend* There is Life After... *to be a part of your personal library as a good read. Once read, I'm sure you will find the courage to take your tragedy and turn it into a triumph.* There is Life After... *is a must-read."*

~ Author SLRandall ~

****

"All of our lives are comprised of bits and pieces of those we choose to role model. This book—comprised of "Life After" experiences, carefully woven together by my lifelong friend—will cause personal reflection and then challenge you to move from your past...forward."

~ Dr. Sharon R. Lidge Brown ~

****

"While Linda's first book, Your Past Has Passed, *is a must-read for any woman yearning to break free of life's chains,* There is Life After... *shows the beauty of what freedom looks like. It completes the process from abolition to reconstruction in a compilation only Linda's sensitivity, experience, and creativity could design!"*

~ Pamela E. Foster, M.S.J., Ph.D., Fellow Author of
My Country: The African Diaspora's Country Music Heritage ~

Dedications

I would like to dedicate this book to my Mom,
Mrs. John T. Hilliard (Louisiana) who is now in Heaven.
My mom met each of her "Life After" experiences with courage and strength. Even at the end of this journey, she was looking forward to her next "Life After…"

I would also like to dedicate this to my Dad, **Rev. John. T. Hilliard**, who, at the age of 91 and after 69 years of marriage, has embarked on his own "Life After" experience. He has accepted that this is not how he'd like it to be, but he's determined to live this "Life After…" with faith, determination, and dignity.

God Bless You Both

There is Life After...

Acknowledgements

I would like to thank all of the people who dedicated their time and efforts to contribute to this project.

To **Tia Jones**, my young cousin who saw my vision and captured it in the book cover. What a talented young lady and a blessing you are!

To my Co-Authors (in no particular order):

Soul Dancer

Toni Dupree

Melissa Secka

Nikki Smith

Lolitha Terry

Dr. Brenda Bradley

Ta-Wanda Wilson

Thank you for sharing your story. We are blessed to be a blessing to someone else, and you all have truly been a blessing to me.

Preface

At one time or another, we all face a "Life After" experience. It can be "Life After" divorce, widowhood, job displacement, or even retirement. It's a time in our lives when something happens that takes us in a new direction in our lives.

After I retired and took stock of my life, I realized that I have had many "Life After" experiences. Some were good; others not so good. But whatever the situation, I not only survived: I came out on the other side a better person. As I began to write these experiences, I realized that everyone has something to share. Not everyone has a book inside of them, but everyone has a "Life After…" story.

Life is a series of events and occurrences. Some of these are planned; others are not. After interviewing several guests on my radio show, *"Phenomenally Yours"*, I realized that people experience their "Life After" journey in different ways. It's not always the storm that resonates, but rather how we come through the storm to the other side. Psalm 30:5 (KJV) reminds us, *"…weeping may endure for a night, but joy comes in the morning"*.

The idea of a collaboration came to me as a way to give people who have a voice a platform to share their testimonies of strength, endurance, and triumph. This collaboration deals with a number of varied "Life After" experiences. It is my hope that the reader will find

There is Life After...

the courage to go on to the next "Life After" journey with anticipation and hope for a better tomorrow.

~ Linda H. Williams ~

Foreword

Life is not life without the different changes and transitions that we undergo—some expected and joyfully received, and others unexpected that often carry their own set of challenges and emotional responses. Each transition comes with an opportunity to learn, grow, and move forward in our lives. However, for many of us, the life circumstances we've endured or suffered through may not have the easiest of outcomes. There is a question, silent or spoke aloud within us: In what way can we emerge from our circumstances, whatever they are, intact, surefooted, and ready to continue and maybe even start over?

We may be hard-pressed to figure out what to do with what we've been dealt. How do we repair a damaged heart or body that has suffered the severe pains of physical and/or emotional abuse from a spouse or family member? In what way can we regain the confidence and self-esteem needed to carry on after being homeless on the streets or after a vicious divorce? What is needed to recover from sexual abuse from a once-trusted and loved family member?

No matter if you've had to pick yourself up after failure, brush off your damaged ego and start all over, or decide *'what now'* upon retirement when your inner voice cries out **"There has to be more!"**, you can rewrite the script and create a new life chapter and a new beginning.

There is Life After…

I am especially excited about being asked to write this Foreword for *There is Life After…* because although my life situation hasn't had the magnitude of tragedy that many of the book's authors have experienced, I've had to alter, adjust, and even change my life direction when faced with personal injuries and chronic pain that set me and my life on a completely new course several times. I've also come to understand—as have the authors you'll meet—that frequently, the most difficult situations lead us in directions we never thought possible. Often, hidden deep within them, are treasures that set us on a new life journey imbued with passion and commitment.

"Life After" is not always easy, and I salute the brave people who've come forward to share their personal truths and even relive the sometimes harrowing, often horrific events, to offer you and all of us hope and strength to move ahead.

I have never met Linda H. Williams personally, although we've been on each other's respective shows and have had numerous conversations, honestly sharing information about our work, lives, and beliefs with one another. I've come to admire and respect Linda's forthrightness, faith, resilience, and spirit, and view her as a powerful teacher and mentor in her own right. I am also amazed and heartened by her ability to forge ahead despite all that she's been through. Her laughter, honesty, and wisdom are refreshing and encouraging. Linda has never let her past defeat her. She has shifted from being homeless, a drunk, a victim of domestic violence, and more, to reinventing herself as an Author, Speaker, Coach, and Show Host committed to the "empowerment and restoration of women".

Linda is a living testament, like the other people in this book, to the power that we all have within us to turn our lives around. They and she demonstrate to every one of us that we can heal, we can set our lives in order, we can redeem ourselves, and we can reclaim our lives and sovereignty. What is amazing is how each of these individuals transformed their "Life After" into something life-altering for themselves and for many others. They turned their grim circumstances into celebrated triumphs.

We can all benefit from their stories and methods that may hold the answer to our own truths and shed light on the amazing beings we truly are. These candid stories will not only inspire you; you will feel uplifted and cheered on by a group of individuals who speak to you, heart-to-heart, and let you know that there can be "Life After" whatever you've been through or are going through right now that has you reeling—and that it's up to you to create a "Life After". However, you don't have to go it alone or suffer silently in shame, regret, or sorrow.

There can be better tomorrows; pain can ease, and forgiveness can replace the deep wounds and anger that may have enveloped you. Even if you feel that you're at an impasse on the road ahead with nowhere to turn, let these stories offer you faith, hope, and courage. Know that within you is the necessary resilience to shift and redefine you. Embrace the growing knowledge that you, too, can push past roadblocks and inertia and forge ahead, restoring dignity and self-affirmation for whatever is to come. You are dynamic and flexible. This means that you have the innate ability to become something else and something more, while you continue to grow in wisdom and assurance. You can revise your life plan and mold yourself into something and someone more beautiful that you are proud to be.

~ *Dr. Jo Anne White* ~

International Best-Selling and Award-Winning Author, Speaker, Certified Coach and Consultant, and Energy Master Teacher who holistically transforms lives and businesses to success and wellness. Dr. White is also the Founder of the *Power Your Life Network* and Executive Host and Producer of the *Power Your Life Shows*.

Connect with Dr. White at:

www.drjoannewhite.com

Introduction

What does your "Life After" look like? For me, I had to deal with "Life After" divorce, after a certain age, homelessness, empty-nesting, and retirement. We all have a life to look forward to after something. It's a time of reflection and regrouping because whatever "it" looks like for you, oftentimes we don't plan on it, so we're not prepared to deal with it. The one thing that's a guarantee about life is that it changes. In the blink of an eye, you can find yourself in a "Life After" situation. Although the situation itself is important in your life, it's how you handle life going forward that determines your success…or failure. The adaptation and reaction to any major change in your life should reveal some key lessons to help cope with whatever your "new" life looks like.

Shift happens—whether we like it or not. Transitions in life are a part of life. For many of us, any kind of change or disruption in our lives can cause anywhere from mild anxiety to total terror. Whether a big change or small, it takes us out of our comfort zone and thrusts us into an area of the unknown. It can range from something that was forced on us, like downsizing or an illness, to an unfortunate but necessary choice, like relocation or becoming a caregiver of a loved-one. We all go through transitions, and those transitions produce those emotional spaces where we have to cut ties with what we know and face a new future.

There is Life After...

The problem that often occurs is that we get stuck in the emotional baggage that comes with change. It's natural to feel anger, sadness, grief, or even to place blame—and that's okay…for a little while. That's when you have your pity party. I often tell clients to have the best pity party they can have for 24 hours. That's it. Twenty-four hours. When the sun comes up, "a new dawn brings a new day". It's time to dust yourself off and figure out how you're going to go on from there. Where do you go from here? When the "old" you has collapsed under the weight of change and you feel unsteady about the "new" you, this is the time to explore, brainstorm, and consider your options.

People often say, *"Get over it"*. Some "Life After" situations are impossible to get over. You never get over the loss of a loved-one. What you have to do is get past it. You have to master the skills necessary for you to work through and continue on to live a life of joy and love. You are not alone and, undoubtedly, you are not the first nor the last that will experience what you're going through. How do you go on "after"? How do you get back on track?

Whether your "Life After" comes from a conscious choice or a circumstance of life, the skills and attitude you need to be successful are the same. You must be positive, patient, and proactive. I have assembled a group of people who have successfully navigated through the rugged road of transition to come out on the other side as a better person—different, but better. It is my hope that somewhere in the pages of their testimony, you will find the courage and determination to press forward to see the ***"joy on the other side of through"***!

Be blessed!

~ Linda H. Williams ~

There is Life After...

TABLE OF CONTENTS

WHAT OTHERS ARE SAYING VI

DEDICATIONS VIII

ACKNOWLEDGEMENTS IX

PREFACE X

FOREWORD XII

INTRODUCTION XVI

CHAPTER ONE 1

    THERE IS "LIFE AFTER..." DIVORCE AND DEPRESSION
    BY: DR. BRENDA BRADLEY

CHAPTER TWO 9

    THERE IS "LIFE AFTER..." EMPTY-NESTING
    BY: LINDA H. WILLIAMS

CHAPTER THREE 15

    THERE IS "LIFE AFTER..." FAILURE
    BY: LINDA H. WILLIAMS

CHAPTER FOUR 23

    THERE IS "LIFE AFTER..." RETIREMENT
    BY: LINDA H. WILLIAMS

CHAPTER FIVE 27

    THERE IS "LIFE AFTER..." PAIN
    BY: LOLITHA Y. TERRY

CHAPTER SIX 35

    THERE IS "LIFE AFTER..." THE APRON
    BY: MELISSA SECKA

CHAPTER SEVEN 45

    THERE IS "LIFE AFTER..." WAITING FOR MANIFESTATION
    BY: NIKKI RUFFIN

CHAPTER EIGHT	49

   THERE IS "LIFE AFTER..." RELEASING THE ILLUSION OF CONTROL
   BY: SOUL DANCER

CHAPTER NINE	55

   THERE IS "LIFE AFTER..." BREAKING THE FAMILY CHAIN
   BY: TA-WANDA WILSON

CHAPTER TEN	63

   THERE IS "LIFE AFTER..." DEVASTATION, HEARTBREAK, LOSS, DEPRESSION, AND SADNESS
   BY: TONI DUPREE

CONCLUSION	69
MEET THE PRESENTER	71
MEET THE AUTHORS	73
(IN ORDER OF APPEARANCE)	73
APPENDIX	84

Chapter One

There is "Life After..." Divorce and Depression

By: Dr. Brenda Bradley

A lot of people get their hearts broken daily. How they cope with the disappointment is another matter entirely. Legendary singer, Al Green, once asked, *"How can you mend a broken heart?"* I experienced heartbreak also—on a massive scale. Thankfully, I survived. For a long time, it seemed my heart would never mend, but it did.

It all started many years ago. I was married to the love of my life. "Keith" and I dated for a while before he finally proposed to me and, of course, I accepted. Later, after we married, he accepted a position overseas. Living overseas was different but exciting. I enjoyed interacting with the nationals and learning their culture. Due to his position, I was a stay-at-home mom and often did volunteer work in the community.

I was happily married, living a comfortable and wonderful life. It didn't get any better than that.

One day, everything took a turn for the absolute worst! Keith called to let me know that he was leaving on a last-minute business trip to Germany. When I arrived home from doing some volunteer work, I noticed a credit report on Keith's desk. That was unusual because he was neat freak and would never leave any papers out. After looking over the report, I placed it back on the desk and proceeded downstairs to grab a drink. Afterwards, I went back upstairs to look at the report again.

That was when I noticed a mortgage for a house that was located in Georgia. I was surprise. Keith and I had never lived in Georgia. I believed it had to be a mistake. I called the mortgage company listed on the report.

"Yes, Mr. Keith Burgess is the co-owner of the house in Georgia", the representative said.

*"Are you **sure**?"* I asked disbelievingly.

"Yes, ma'am."

"Can you send me a proof of ownership and other relating documents?"

"Of course, ma'am. All I need is the address to send it to."

Two weeks later, I received the proof. It was true: My husband had purchased a home with another woman. I could not believe it. I was pissed! Had I been living a lie? I chose to wait until the papers came prior to confronting him.

With sadness, I waited until he returned from work. When he entered, he greeted me, but I just couldn't answer.

"Hey, darling! Are you okay?"

I walked towards him. *"Keith, I was checking through the credit report today and I saw something unbelievable."*

"What is it?"

"I saw a mortgage for a house in Georgia." I watched his face as I spoke. It was very obvious that he knew exactly what I was talking about. I wanted to cry, but forced myself to continue. *"I thought it was a mistake, so I called the company listed to confirm. I was told that you are the co-owner of the house with another woman. I have the proof here, Keith."* I raised the document and showed it to him.

His expression totally changed to something I had never seen before. It was downright evil. **"How dare you touch my things!"** he shouted.

I was shocked. **"Keith, I am your damn wife!"**

"I don't give a damn! You had no right to touch things that belong to me!"

"Who is the woman, Keith?"

He got really mad and cursed at me. It was a side of him I had never imagined I would see. I told him I was giving him two weeks to send me back to the United States. I packed my bags. We did not speak again.

I decided to leave him and figure out what exactly I was going to do. My mind never went to divorce because I loved him. When I left him, I only took two suitcases and a car. I had to get a job and be independent again. I couldn't believe that my life would turn out the way it did. I actually believed in happily-ever-after. I never thought I would be separated from the man I loved.

Six months after leaving, Keith served me with divorce papers. I had just found a job around that time. I was both furious and hurt. I could not believe this was happening.

I didn't have much money, but I soon found a lawyer I could afford and who was eager to take my case. My lawyer seemed to be a determined woman. I was glad to have her on my side.

My hopes were dashed away when one day, I received a call from my lawyer. *"Mrs. Burgess, I need to see you immediately."*

I picked up my bag, got permission to leave my job, and went to see her. When I arrived, she asked me to have a seat.

"What is it?" I asked.

"I am so sorry, Brenda", she began. *"You lost everything a judge would have awarded you because when your husband married you, he was already married."*

My heart seemed to stop when I heard that. Keith was already married to another woman when he married me? It was too much for me to handle. It was the worst betrayal I have ever experienced.

"This wife of his…what's her name?" I asked.

"Deborah Burgess."

I had already guessed. It was the same woman whose name was the other co-owner of the house on the document that was sent to me. Keith had a house with his wife. I cried in the lawyer's office and she comforted me.

I could not return to work and don't know how I managed to get home, either. I lost my way, my job, and my mentality. I was dying inside and when I sought treatment, I was diagnosed with severe depression and placed under the care of both a psychiatrist and psychologist.

I was medicated for over a year. There were times when I contemplated suicide. The only reason I didn't do it was because of my children. During this period, my life was miserable. My bills fell behind. I got jobs but couldn't keep them for long. I felt abandoned and lonely. I had lost my way.

I would often cry myself to sleep at night and wondered why God had allowed all of this to happen to me. I never turned my back on God, but I was left feeling as though He no longer found favor in me. One day, while in a store, this older lady walked up to me and told me that whatever is going on in my life, to just hold on and believe it will come to pass. That following Sunday, I found enough strength to go to church. While in church, I felt the presence of the Spirit wrap His arms around me. From that day forward, I believed again.

The journey to "find myself" was treacherous and quite difficult. I spent a lot of time trying to reconnect and make sense of the pain and suffering. After developing a spiritual relationship, I learned to love again; however, this time, I loved me first.

Several years after my divorce was finalized, I bumped into Keith. We were both quite surprised to see one another. By then, I was already a changed person—in many ways.

"How have you been?" he asked.

"Fine, thanks", I replied. I was surprised that I didn't hate him as much as I did before.

"You look good."

"Thanks."

"Can I treat you to dinner? I just want to talk", he said.

"Of course, Keith."

I accepted because it gave me a chance to close this painful chapter of my life. I had been depressed for so long, and this was a chance to really put everything totally behind me.

There is Life After…

At dinner, we talked about our lives together and our lives apart. I found out that he was now back with his first wife and they had a daughter together. He asked for forgiveness, and I forgave him in all totality. I was able to close that chapter of my life for good. No baggage.

It has been over 14 years since that traumatic experience left me with a broken heart. There were many dark and painful days. Looking back, I can truly say that without the grace of God, I know I would not have made it.

Today, I am in a wonderful and meaningful relationship. My life is on track and much better than before.

There is a saying: *"As long as there is life, there is hope."* No matter the problems we face—be it depression, betrayal, or any other heartbreaking thing—there is still hope.

I faced divorce and depression, but I also found out that *"There is Life After…"* them.

Linda H. Williams

Chapter Two

There is "Life After…" Empty-Nesting

By: Linda H. Williams

All the children are grown and gone. How do I fill the many hours that I used to spend with them? Homework, after-school activities, long talks about life… What do I do now? Empty-Nest Syndrome is described as "a sense of loneliness parents feel when their children grow up and leave home for the first time for college or to live on their own".

We spend our entire lives taking care of other people. We are born nurturers, and some of us do it quite well! We become the 'Soccer Mom', the 'Scout Mom', and the 'Cheerleader Mom'. Then, one day, we look up and someone else has taken those positions. Our children have outgrown those activities and moved on to the next chapter in their lives that no longer involve us.

I remember when my youngest son first left home. He went to spend the summer with his older brother before heading off to college. There was a sense of relief, but underlying that relief was also a little sadness. The last thing he said to me was, *"Mom, you know I won't be back to live with you anymore, right?"* I replied rather flippantly, *"I hope not!"* Then we laughed and hugged and I said, *"See ya later!"*

Once I arrived home, though, the sense that I had lost something was very real.

In a column titled *Saying Goodbye To My Child, The Youngster*, published recently in the Washington Post, writer Michael Gerson wrote that dropping his eldest son off at college was the worst thing that time had done to him.

"With due respect to my son's feelings, I have the worse of it. I know something he doesn't—not quite a secret, but incomprehensible to the young," he wrote. "He is experiencing the adjustments that come with beginnings. His life is starting for real.
I have begun the long letting go."

I couldn't agree more. Letting go of anything is hard, but letting go of someone you've known and loved even before they took their first breath is difficult. I admit: I purposely taught my sons to be independent. It was important that they be leaders and not followers. As such, making the decision to attend college out of state was a natural thing for them. It was finally their time to spread their wings and fly. In doing so, it leaves those of us (who gave them wings) to watch them fly away.

In the past, research suggested that parents dealing with 'Empty-Nest Syndrome' experienced a profound sense of loss that might make them vulnerable to depression, alcoholism, identity-crisis, and marital conflicts. However, recent studies suggest that an empty nest might reduce work and family conflicts, and can provide parents with many other benefits. When the last child leaves home, parents have a new opportunity to reconnect with each other, improve the quality of their marriage, and rekindle interests for which they previously might not have had time.

But what happens if you're a single parent? What are you supposed to do now?

I spent most of my parenting life raising my two sons. Sometimes, there was a dad in our home, but for a long time, it was my sons and me. I recall a client who raised her daughter as a single parent. They became best friends in addition to the mother/daughter relationship. After graduating from high school, the daughter accepted a scholarship to attend college in another state. Of course, her mother was proud and ecstatic. They continued that bond that had been established throughout the years, and my client didn't really experience that "empty nest" feeling. She left her daughter's bedroom exactly as it had been when she occupied it—fully expecting her daughter to return home after college to pick up where they left off. Fortunately, my client's daughter was offered a very lucrative position upon graduation in another state, which she accepted. My client was simultaneously proud and devastated. Her question to me was, *"What am I supposed to do now? I've spent my entire life dedicated to my daughter, and now she's moved on without me"*.

Unfortunately, many of us single parents fall into this category. I stood in my son's room and felt a deep sense of loss. Life as I had known it was gone. I had to discover my own "Life After…" Of course, I still had my job to occupy my days, but what about the evenings? Having a son meant that we didn't sit on the bed at night and share details about our day, but he was still in the house. Even when he went out with his friends, I knew he'd be coming home. Now, he had a new home away from home.

It wasn't quite as bad when my older son left because I still had the youngest, and he was several years younger than his older brother. It was the day I put my youngest son on the airplane that I realized I had to create my own "Life After…" So, after a while, I put on my big girl panties and set about discovering who I am and what my purpose is outside of being a good mom.

It's been 14 years since that day. I've discovered quite a lot about myself. You see, this should be a time for some introspection. All of the normal distractions of being a mom are gone. It's time to take stock of yourself. I discovered my strengths and my weaknesses; my good, bad, and ugly. It hasn't always been pleasant, but being alone doesn't mean being lonely. I've actually discovered that I have a pretty good relationship with myself!

That's what "Life After Empty-Nesting" should be about: a time to discover yourself, applaud yourself, and improve yourself. This is not a time to brood about everything you gave up for your children. If you sacrificed yourself for your children, then you were a good parent. I found the courage to ask my sons, *"What kind of mom was I?"* Having been an alcoholic and a victim of domestic violence, I had my own issues that were consuming me. It was important for me to know how my sons remembered me as they were growing up.

Both of my sons told me that even with all of the "mess" going on in my life, I was the absolute **BEST** Mom.

What a marvelous way to begin my "Life After…"!

Linda H. Williams

Chapter Three

There is "Life After…" Failure

By: Linda H. Williams

Everybody fails at something at some point in their lives. It may be a failing grade at school, a failure to get that promotion on your job, or you may fail at love. Success and failure are two sides of the same coin. Although you wish to experience only successes and no failures, you can't have one without the other. Failure, like success, is a fact of life. It is always lurking just around the corner, and you have no choice but to learn to deal with failure if you are to be successful.

How do **you** define failure? What do you consider a failure? Is there something you didn't do well, or perhaps your dream went south with all of your hopes? Failure is not necessarily a lack of success, but rather the inability to do what you can do in the best way you can. Thinking of yourself as a failure can become an unintentional habit—those times that you count small setbacks as an identifier of failure. Sometimes, you define yourself as a failure when you simply indulge yourself in laziness.

Do you fail sometimes? Yes, but your failure is simply a lack of the necessary insight to do the best you can do. A major part of getting past your past is acceptance. When you finally learn to accept that failure is a part of life, you can begin to take the next step in your journey called 'life'. Life is full of unexpected events; some good and some bad. You have to learn how to build on the positives and learn from the negatives.

Many people think failure is an unwanted end of something that they tried to do, when in actuality, it's just the beginning. At some point in all of our lives, we have failed and something. As such, it would be easy to think of ourselves as failures. Great achievers don't give up; they keep on trying. They hold onto a self-belief and don't allow their failures to become their focal point. It is impossible for you to move forward if you believe you are a failure. You have to be able to separate life's unfortunate events from your self-worth and your future actions. Successful people are not immune to failure. It is how they process it and what they do about the failure that makes the difference.

What separates people who enjoy success from the majority who end up never getting what they want is how they respond to failure. It is not that successful people don't fail or haven't failed at something. It is what you do about failure that makes a big difference.

There are three common ways that you can respond to failure.

Do you make excuses, lay blame, and give up? Are you one of those people who constantly whine when they don't get their way? Do you come up with a hundred different excuses as to why something didn't work out like you thought it would? Do you always find someone else to blame your misfortune on?

How many times have you said something like the following to yourself?

It's not fair.

I'm too young.

I'm too old.

If you are in this group, you will ultimately feel frustrated at your repeated attempts and subsequent failures. Eventually, you will give up. You will settle into mediocrity and resign yourself to the belief that everything you want is out of your reach.

Do you keep trying the same thing over and over again? If so, you have a lot more determination than if you were in the first group, but the outcome is generally the same. When you don't get the desired outcome, you won't quit; you'll jump right back into action. Do you think your failure was a result of not trying hard enough?

Do you think to yourself…?

*If I just keep on trying and try a little harder, surely,
I will eventually succeed.*

No matter how many times you fail, you will just keep trying harder and harder. If you are in this group, it is possible for you to accomplish some of your goals. If you set small, incremental goals, with enough time and effort, you may eventually succeed. If, on the other hand, you set exceptional goals, like opening your own business, you will not be successful by simply trying over and over again. If you keep using the same approach, you will keep getting the same results. People in this group can be so dogged in their pursuits that they fail to see that the actions they think will produce the desired results are actually sabotaging their efforts.

Do you get feedback, change your strategy, and take action until you succeed? If you are in this category, you have a different perception of failure. You see it as an opportunity to grow. You tend to look into the failure and derive feedback so that you can change your strategy the next time. If the initial strategy was insufficient or you didn't take enough action, you will use this feedback to change your tactics and try again. If you still don't succeed, repeat the analysis, get feedback, and take another approach until you get what you want. Of course, if you are in this group, you tend to be more realistic so as to minimize permanent failure. This group views failure as life trying to teach them a lesson. Life is about lessons. Until you learn them, you will continually make the same mistake. So, remember that every time you don't get what you want, it is life giving you feedback. It is this continuous feedback that you need to help adjust your approach until you reach your goal.

Getting your life back on track after a failure is not always an easy task. You have to look at life differently in order to motivate yourself back into action.

How do you look at things differently?

You have to know your limits. What are your strengths and weaknesses? If you want to reduce your chances of making the same mistakes as before, you have to know what you can and cannot do. You want to set goals that will challenge you to reach for higher heights, but you don't want to stress yourself out. Challenging yourself can sometimes help to identify your limitations. There is always room for improvement. You were born with a gift, and it's a part of your journey to discover what that is.

Stop comparing yourself. It's natural to compare yourself with someone you think either has it "more together" or that you feel is in worse shape than you are. What we don't know is what their "story" is. Do you want to experience what they did in order to be in the position they're in? Sometimes, you can concentrate on other people's success and not even realize that it only torments your spirit to the point that you can lose your passion and confidence in the things that you are good at. We are created equal, but you have your own strengths and abilities. We are instructed in Galatians 6:4 (NIV), *"Let each one prove what his own work is, and then he will have cause for exultation in regard to himself alone, and not in comparison with the other person"*.

Don't let the expectations of others define your success. The expectations of our immediate family members, friends, teachers, coworkers, and others should only be considered if they coincide with your own expectations. Sometimes, it becomes a hindrance to your growth as a person to base your capabilities on someone else's definition. As a result, you end up trying to please people. People-pleasers never find true success and are usually unable to bounce back from failure. Learn to be yourself. Let your true colors shine through.

Be realistic. You have to be a strong enough person to face your biggest mistakes and their consequences. It takes a stronger person to admit that they didn't do something right and move on than to blame themselves forever for being a total failure. Look at the situation and try to sort things out. What did you do right? What went wrong? Doing better the next time and not making the same mistakes is as simple as that. Remember that your failures and mistakes don't define you, and they surely don't make you a lesser person.

Stop taking yourself so seriously. You have to find the humor in life—from the simple things all the way up to the complex—despite all of the chaos. You should live your life so that you have something to laugh about every day. Does it bother you when people laugh at you? Of course, it does! It bothers everyone! If what you did was funny, laugh with them. It's better to have someone to laugh with than to go through life with no laughter at all.

Share yourself. You would be amazed at how brightening up a person's day by sharing positive thoughts can actually brighten your own life. You really do reap what you sow. Give a little love, and it all comes back to you. Don't just sit there pondering life's failures.

Sometimes, you have to be the one to get involved and explore all the possibilities that life has to offer. Be a blessing to others. Just go and have a life!

Seize the day. We have to learn how to live each day as if it is our last and to count our blessings every day—literally. It is the only way we can appreciate how marvelous the gift of life is.

Still... Failure is painful, right? Successful people would disagree. To them, failure is a part of winning, and their sense of value is not dependent on the wins or the failures. You have to develop beliefs that will allow you to take advantage of negatives and turn them into your advantages.

I found an article that has 10 rules to live by to turn your failure into success (James, 2012):

1. Failure renews my humility, sharpens my objectivity, and makes me more resilient.
2. I take the challenge seriously, but I do not take myself too seriously.
3. The more I fail, the more I succeed; and then failure is a part of the process of achieving my objectives.
4. Failure is temporary when I use it as an opportunity to try new ideas.
5. I learn more from failure than from success.

6. Negative feedback is information that helps me correct my course so that I stay on target.
7. I am paid for the number of times I fail.
8. My self-esteem is not based on the reactions of others, but on my own sense of virtue.
9. The unkindness of others reminds me that I need to be kind to myself.
10. It takes courage to fail, because nobody ever got ahead without taking risks.

"There are always challenges at every stage in our lives. Overcoming them is what life is all about."

What separates successful people from those who never seem to get what they want is how they respond to failure. Failure is a natural part of life. It is crazy to thing you will succeed at everything you do. It's what you do with those failures that ultimately make the difference in your "Life After Failure".

Chapter Four

There is "Life After..." Retirement

By: Linda H. Williams

We wake up every morning for 40 years preparing to go to work. For some, it's a chore; for those of us fortunate enough to love our jobs, it's a joy. Whatever the case, it's a structure. What happens when you wake up on that first Monday morning of retirement and you have nowhere to go? Some of us enter retirement with a full-blown plan. Other new retirees struggle to fill a blank canvas. What am I going to do with all of this free time? A retirement plan is not just about having enough money to live comfortably. It is also about figuring out how you want to spend all your newfound free time. Now is the time to ask yourself, *"What do I want to be when I grow up?"*

The key to a meaningful retirement is not just filling your time, but finally pursuing your passions that are based on what's important to you. Your job or your work is what you do, not who you are. Your retirement is an opportunity to create a life that reflects more closely who you are. It's a time to think about all of those things that you put off doing for yourself. What did you dream about doing when you were little and someone asked you, *"What do you want to be when you grow up?"* That's sometimes easier said than done. With so many choices and so much freedom, figuring out what you value most can be tough. When I retired, I had this plan on what I would do. It's fortunate for me that I was already on a path of pursuing what I was passionate about, but without the structure that work had provided me, it was difficult to accomplish anything. The first week went by, and I had not accomplished one thing!

I spent the last 20 years rising at 4:30 a.m. to begin my day. For the first six months after retirement, I still woke up at that hour. The **only** difference was I didn't have to get up, so I took that time for my daily meditation. The normal routine is working five days a week, using that 6th day to take care of your business, and Sunday is spent worshipping and preparing to start the process over again on Monday morning. So, of course, that first Sunday of retirement, my mindset was on what I had to do to get ready for Monday morning. When the realization hit that I didn't have to do that, I had an initial sense of relief and joy.

I was blessed that I had a plan and had actually begun working on it. I was a freelance writer and had a job of writing a weekly article for an online magazine that was due on Friday. It was normal for me to have the article completed and submitted by Wednesday. Thursday of my first week of retirement rolled around, and I had not even started on the article! Where had the week gone? What had I been doing all week? That's when I realized that what had been normal for the past 40 years was no longer the norm. I had to create a "new norm".

Unfortunately, a lot of people who retire can't seem to create that much-needed 'new norm'. That's why we hear of so many people working their entire lives and then dying within a year of retirement.

My next dilemma was: How do I create a 'new norm' after 40 years? After decades of following someone else's rules, it was a relief to be able to follow my own. The problem was this: I really didn't have any rules of my own to follow. It's easy to feel lost, fearful, or sad when reaching this important milestone. You logically know that you are retiring from work—not life—but it doesn't always feel that way. There is only so much cleaning you can do before your house is spotless.

With some retirees living well into their 90s, that's a lot of days to fill with something meaningful. Now is the time to do something that you want to do. "Life After Retirement" can be anything you want it to be. You have earned the freedom to chart your own course; but with freedom comes responsibility. No one is going to tell you how to get the most from "Life After" the age of sixty. It's up to you to decide which passions to pursue, which people to have in your life, and which places to visit.

For me, it was time to begin to chart the course for the next chapter in my life. Even with a vision, it was not always an easy journey. What I thought I wanted to do wasn't in God's plan. Once His plan was revealed in my life, I didn't think He was moving fast enough! I now had the time to wait on Him.

Habakkuk 2:3 (NIV) says, *"For still the vision awaits its appointed time; it hastens to the end—it will not lie. If it seems slow, wait for it; it will surely come; it will not delay"*. While I was working for someone else's vision, I didn't have time to wait. Now that I was pursuing my vision, I had the time but not the patience. Retirement has taught me that I don't have to be in a hurry anymore for anything. I've even slowed my spirit down to wait patiently in the never-ending lines we find ourselves in these days.

Retirement is a wonderful thing. I've grown to a new dimension within myself since retiring. It's now time to do what fulfills you; what makes you happy. Find your purpose. Pursue your passion. How do you find your passion? Think about what you love to do and would gladly do, even if you weren't getting paid. Your passion lies there. Do you love to cook? What about decorating? Do you have a knack for making your home look like it should be in a magazine? That's your passion. Now, it's time to work on you and, if you're fortunate, your passion will turn a profit.

Don't waste time thinking about past mistakes and missed opportunities.

Today is the first day of the rest of your life. Enjoy!

Chapter Five

There is "Life After…" Pain

By: Lolitha Y. Terry

As I began writing my portion of this anthology, I didn't really see myself as someone who had achieved much. However, after reading what I wrote, I realize not only am I an overcomer; I am more than a Conqueror. I am more than a Survivor. **I am Victorious!**

Many can't say they would have made it through what I have. There were days I thought I wouldn't live to see another day, yet I have seen so much that I am thankful for. I am very proud of all the opportunities that have been given me because I never thought in a *million* years that I'd be where I am today. You see, with a mental disease called 'depression', you never know what the days hold. I fought this disease for many years, but decided I would not let it take away my chance to live a normal, happy, productive life.

It was only a short time ago while praying, I found myself really experiencing pain like never before. I know in life, we all go through pain, whether it's the pain of heartbreak, the pain of illnesses, the pain of loss and death, the pain of divorce and breakup, the pain of losing a job, the pain of failure, or sometimes even simple disagreements can cause the ache of pain. I've experienced all of these pains at some point in my life. Each time I've felt the pain, I found myself successfully dealing with it. Eventually, it would pass and I would move on…or so I thought.

On this particular evening, while praying to God, I felt past pains resurfacing. I wept uncontrollably. I found myself in somewhat of a panic attack. I laid down on the floor and began to deeply breathe. For about five minutes, I just took small breaths to calm myself. While I still wept—albeit a bit more silently—I was able to gather myself. Finally, I asked God, *"Where did all of **that** come from?"* God spoke silently, yet in such a sweet voice. *"I allowed you to see what you hadn't identified or accepted. It is only when you identify and accept your pain that I can help you heal from your pain!"*

You see, all of those years I thought "it" was over and I'd just move on was really me pushing the pain under the rug. It was in that moment of breakdown that I had finally come to terms with where I was in life! I had come a long way. As far back as I could remember, I've never ever been really happy. I was always rebellious, making bad choices, in and out of wrong relationships, and always desperate to keep up with the façade of being happy (whatever I thought happiness was). I never really tapped into what true happiness meant. I never understood that real happiness is a choice. The only way I could move into a life that was filled with love, joy, and peace was for me to find the love of God first within myself. I had to learn how to love me!

There is Life After...

All of my young adult life, I played the happiness role—and I even fooled some people. I was never truly happy with myself. I was taught not to deal with issues in life that will cause pain. I, like many, was taught to be strong and keep it moving. Sometimes, however, the pain in life is so crippling that it seems impossible to move beyond the crippling emotions. Emotions sometimes get the best of us. I thought I needed to appear stronger than I actually was. You can probably relate. We hide behind the pain and we live a lifetime of sedating the pain as opposed to really dealing with it and healing from it.

While on the floor praying that day, I chose to deal with the pains of my past. As I began to call out the pains that were holding me captive, I had to allow God to show me what the actual root of the pain was. I had been calling out the symptoms of the pain, which were anger, unforgiveness, jealousy, etc. I realized then that I needed to call out the root of the pain. Where did it all stem from?

At the time of this writing, I am 48 years old and, for the first time in my life, I'm at a happy place in life; yet, at that moment, I had unresolved issues that were still painful and were holding me back from my true peace. I couldn't move into my purpose and I would never be able to experience prosperity and power because the pain of the past was still there. So, instead of dealing with just the symptoms, I had to be willing to go to the root and tell God everything that was hurting me—**and I had to be honest!**

Yes, of course God knew, but He wanted to hear it from me! He wanted me to embrace it and acknowledge: **I AM HURTING!** That would be the only way to surrender it to Him. I had to trust that after I yelled, screamed, cried, shouted, and rolled over on the floor telling God how angry I was about my hurts and the people who had caused them, I also had to be ready to accept the responsibility of how I had hurt myself. Self-inflicted pain can sometimes be worse than pains from others. I could no longer blame anyone else.

I was truly feeling the pain of my past. The feelings of not being a good mother to my older twins began to surface. The hurt of not being where I wanted to be in life was showing its face. The "should've, could've, would'ves" were *plaguing* me. I was discouraged because of my age and afraid that I had wasted so much time, I wouldn't live to enjoy the great blessings of God. I was angry because I was financially broke and my parents hadn't taught me anything about finances. I was angry because I had stayed in a relationship for 12 years and was heartbroken that it had ended. I was angry that my marriage had ended and I was facing divorce. I waited 40 years to be married, and it ended in six. I was hurting because my business wasn't doing what it needed to do. It seemed that everyone in my company was excelling except me, and although I hadn't spent enough time taking my business seriously and building it, I felt that I should have still been further along than I was.

My life is my testimony! Not realizing what that anger was doing to me, I had three heart attacks in one day! I was rushed to the hospital and had stents placed in my heart, only to find out I was diabetic. It was so much to have gone through at such a young age. I was hurting over friendship issues, family issues, job-related issues, children issues, health issues, business issues, and financial issues that led me to bankruptcy. I just knew that going through all of that would kill me for sure. I think it's safe to say that I had a lot of unresolved hurt; a lot of issues that God knew I needed to surrender to Him. I could only do that when I embraced the truth, embraced the pain, and acknowledged the pain.

I've had to dig…and dig deeply. How did I get to peace, purpose, prosperity, and power? I started to seek God **FIRST**! Oftentimes, we try so hard to handle things on our own, but there is *NO WAY* I would have made it without connecting myself to a source higher than myself. I began to clean the toxins from my mindset through meditation and affirmations. I studied the Law of Attraction and how it aligns with the Word of God and began to apply it to my everyday life. I had to separate myself from people, places, and things that hindered me.

What I am telling you did not come without pain, tears, and much sacrifice. It was not a quick fix. There were days that I grew very weary; other days, I felt nothing I did was working for me. I almost gave up on myself, but I continued to pray and asked God to help me! I would cry and look at my daughter's picture. I wanted so badly to just get up for **HER**, and I ***DID***! She became my **WHY**! I dug deep, pushed, and began to meditate day in and day out. I recited affirmations and believed them. I prayed and fasted. I set goals that I could attain without becoming so overwhelmed, and I took steps towards my goals day by day.

There are four things I did when I made up my mind that I wanted to be a *WINNER* in life:

1. I surrendered to God and trusted His plan for my life. I am nothing without God. Everything that I am and everything that I've done and will do is solely because of **HIM** and His plan for my life.
2. I take time every day to acknowledge where I am. Every day will not render you the best that you are always hoping for, but no matter what the day brings, it does not determine who you are! God created you and knew the plan He had for your life before you were born. Yes, there have been challenges. Yes, there are times when I wanted to just throw in the towel. Yes, there were times when I didn't get the support I needed from family or friends. Instead of quitting, I cried out to God for help, and He sent the right people who were designed to be placed on my path that would help me get to my destiny.
3. I stopped comparing myself to everyone else! Once I stopped comparing myself to others, I was able to focus on the assignment that God has given me. You are unique! It doesn't matter who is doing what you are doing; God created you to do it to the best of your ability—and you will succeed at doing it! Take your eyes off of others. Stay in your lane. I am now in

my lane! I am winning by staying in my lane. Fast or slow, I'm competing with no one but myself.

4. **NEVER GIVE UP!** My breakthrough has come because I did not give up.

I have witnessed the hand of God moving in my life and can honestly say that the brokenness has since come together. Whatever you may be going through today, there is hope and "Life After..." You've survived this long, which lets me know that there is a Divine Purpose for your life. Reach up to your Higher Power, Universe, God, or whatever your Source may be, and connect. Your better days are ahead. All it takes is your decision to *LIVE*!

So, to all those who read my story, know that you, too, are able to **WIN**! Of course, it's not easy. Nothing worthwhile is easy. However, you are not your situation. You are not your circumstances. You are Victorious! You are a Conqueror!

I encourage you today: Let go of your yesterdays and walk confidently towards your happy "Life After..."!

Linda H. Williams

Chapter Six

There is "Life After..." The Apron

By: Melissa Secka

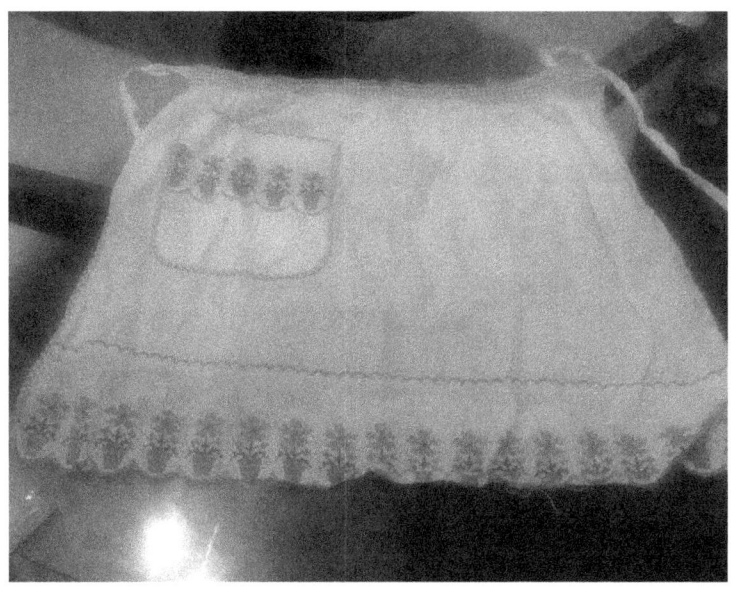

I remember my grandmother wiping her hands on the white apron with red flowers. She said, *"You know I'm not your mother"*. I guess it was no big deal to her, but I was only eight years old. **What was she talking about? Of course, she was my mother; she was all I had known!** She continued rolling the dough for her bread as if she'd just asked me how my day at school went. I remember feeling angry. I soon stopped calling her 'mother' and began to call her by her name: Lucy.

My aunt was the only one who took the time to explain to me that my birth mother didn't want her "black" children; she only kept the "high-yella" ones. I did have a hero in my grandfather, though. He gave me anything I asked for. He would often tell me how jealous Lucy was of me. He was so mean and hateful towards my grandmother. It was no secret that he hated her. The home in which I grew up was very abusive. My grandfather was a weekend drinker, and I grew to hate Friday through Sunday. We all knew we had to run from him and his guns when he was drunk.

At about the age of nine, my breasts started to develop…but there was something wrong: I had two on one side and one on the other. In my nine-year-old mind, I must have been a bad person. First, I learned the woman who I thought was my mother really wasn't, and then came the deformed breasts.

The following memory is as clear as if it happened just today…

My grandmother left me home on February 4th, 1978. She wanted me to go to the laundromat with her, but I didn't want to go. I thought, *"I don't want to change out of my nightgown and I surely don't want to wash anyone's dirty clothes"*. I should have gone with her.

There is Life After...

My grandfather came in drunk (as usual) and asked me to comb his hair. We all liked to comb his hair, but he especially liked the way I did it. This time was going to be different, though. He wasn't angry like he usually was when he got drunk, so I quickly ran and got the comb, sat on the bed, and began to comb his pretty hair. The vibe was different, though. Something didn't feel right in my spirit. He suddenly said, *"Come here and let me suck them three little titties you got"*. He aggressively lifted up my gown and began to suck my breasts. It hurt and I asked him to please stop, but he wouldn't. I wanted him to stop but instead, he sat me on the hot heater and began to choke me. Then, he raped me! When he was done with his business with me, he gave me five dollars and told me not to tell anyone; it was going to be "our little secret".

When my grandmother came home, I ran out of the house to my uncles' house and told them what happened. They responded by saying, *"What goes on in our home stays in our home"*. This was also the first time my grandmother **ever** laid her hands on me. She slapped me and told me to **STOP** telling that lie. She knew, though. I know she knew.

My mother took me to the hospital and the doctors confirmed the sexual assault. My aunt told me, *"Keep this in the family. Remember what your grandmother told you"*. I couldn't believe half of my family thought I was lying, while the other half wanted to keep everything a family 'secret'.

I remember when I was 14, the man I grew up thinking was my dad told me he wasn't my biological father. This man took me to church and everything, but he never quite got around to adopting me. **Who did I belong to? Did anybody want me?**

After that revelation, I suffered from depression and became very suicidal. I developed very destructive behaviors and began cutting myself in an attempt to relieve some of my internal pain. No one believed I was raped by my grandfather because he—whom everyone adored—had convinced them I was making up a story just to get attention. So, I got picked on and teased; not quite the attention I wanted.

I was introduced to "Mary Jane" (street slang for marijuana) and Acid (another 'recreational' drug) about this time. I was at a house party where everyone else was doing it, so I gave it a try. That was not a good idea at all, especially with my low self-esteem and self-destructive behavior. Naturally, I overindulged and, as a result, I had my first nervous breakdown. No one was there for me. No one cared about what I was going through or what happened to me. As a matter-of-fact, those who should have been there for me actually made my life worse. The adults allowed other family members to call me names like 'Fruitcake', 'Crazy', and 'Liar'.

The only person I ever remember being there for me was Mrs. Padgett (one of my 12th grade teachers). I finally had someone in my life who cared about me. I told her what happened with my grandfather and shared that I was considering quitting school to become a prostitute, but Mrs. Padgett took the time to talk to me and encouraged me to graduate. I didn't know anything about college, even though there was a well-respected college right up the road from the small town I grew up in. No one ever told me about nor pushed me to attend college. Well, I did graduate, but no one celebrated with me. **SO WHAT!**

At the age of 17, I joined Job Corps and relocated to Atlanta. ***I TRIED TO RUN FROM MY FEELINGS, BUT THEY SOMEHOW KEPT FOLLOWING ME (LOL!).*** I was living life with the notion that no one cared about me; yet I didn't know how to care for myself and lived life with no boundaries. The expected happened: I got pregnant. Then, the unexpected happened: I lost the baby. That prompted my second nervous breakdown. In May of that year, my grandmother and mother came to Atlanta to pick me up and take me back home.

Upon my return, I quickly noticed nothing had changed since my departure those many months prior. It was as if time had stood completely still. Everyone was still doing and saying the same things to me, except it was worse because I had gotten pregnant, miscarried, and had *another* nervous breakdown. Everybody really thought I was full-blown crazy for sure! I couldn't stay there. I had to **GO**!

So, in July of that year, I moved back to Atlanta. I was **STILL** trying to run away from myself, so I began using cocaine and became very promiscuous. I tried to do whatever I could to take my mind off of the pain of my reality. I didn't care about acquiring AIDS or any other debilitating disease; I just wanted to die! I didn't die, but I did meet all kinds of people while living in that lifestyle.

At the age of 22, I met and married a man who, even though he was in a wheelchair, had money—or so I thought. Boy, was I wrong! Not only did he **NOT** have any money, he was mean and abusive. After he hit me one time, I got so angry, drove him to a bridge, pushed him out of the car, and left him on the side of the bridge with his dripping Jeri Curl hairstyle! The only good thing that came out of that marriage was my son. (The doctor said that after the rape, I would never get pregnant—or if I did, I would not be able to carry full-term. Thank God, I knew a little bit about Jesus! I gave birth to a six-pound, five-ounce baby boy!) Eventually, I left my Jeri Curl husband and moved back home to North Carolina. I never divorced him, but he later died. Good riddance.

Some time later, I moved back to Atlanta with my son. I was then introduced to heroin and moved in with a man who was 13 years my senior. Except for the first two weeks we were together, he beat me **EVERY** day…for eight years. Today, I still wear the scars. In a way, I thought the mistreatment was expected and right. After all, it's what I saw my grandmother endure. She advised me in this way: *"As long as he pays the bills, stay."* Since I didn't have any money, I did just that: stayed. What other choice did I have?

I had no idea my son knew what was going on at the time. When he got older, he told me about how he would sit outside of our bedroom door and hear that man beating on me…*every day*. He even admitted to me that he once put a BB gun to his head planning to kill himself. **What was I doing to my baby?** ***Oh my God!***

After one violent episode when that man beat me with a hammer, I finally mustered up the courage to fight back and stand up for myself. I thought he was going to kill me that time for sure. I don't know if I operated more out of fear or anger, but I fought back. That was the straw that broke the camel's back. It was time to leave.

I at least had sense enough to realize my son needed a more stable environment, so we went back to North Carolina to live for a while. When I tired of 'home' and the "same-old-same-old", I kissed my son good-bye with the prayer on my lips that his life would gain the stability I so desired for him, and I moved back to Atlanta—back to my old ways and habits: substance abuse and promiscuity. I met a man with this new thing called 'crack'. *Hmm…What is this 'crack thing'?* It was good to me, and so was that wonderful man. I ended up moving in with him. He provided me just the opportunity I needed to leave that older, abusive man. I finally had someone in my life who loved me.

That lasted for about a year. Crack became my "main squeeze". That was all I needed and wanted.

I watched a movie on Lifetime that showed women suing their fathers for raping them. **What? You mean to tell me I might be able to get some money for what my grandfather did to me?** There is no statute of limitation in North Carolina as it relates to sex crimes, so I got an attorney and sued my grandfather. I won the case! I received $7,000.00—and went straight to the crack house.

I lost **EVERYTHING** in the blink of an eye. I was smoking up to $500.00 a ***DAY***! I was doing whatever I had to get that next high when the money ran out. I had moved into an extended-stay motel and smoked so much crack, the neighbors began to complain to the manager. When the manager came to talk to me about the "situation", I had sex with him to keep from getting put out.

On July 10th, 1998, I locked myself in a motel room and smoked from dusk to dawn. At around 3:00 a.m., the two guys I had loaned my car to came in. I knew they were going to rape me (and possibly kill me). I kept right on getting high. I then took one "good hit"…and then **EVERYTHING** went grey. I began to lose control of my bodily functions. I knew I was about to die a horrible death when I heard the distant sound of my son's voice say, ***"My momma overdosed on crack!"*** I began to see myself falling into *HELL*— literally. I cried out to God: *"PLEASE, LET ME LIVE!"* Immediately, I was sober. I looked over and saw the two guys fast asleep, almost as if they were *DEAD*. One of them had my car keys laying in his hand. I grabbed the keys, then drove to my friend's house.

That was my new beginning.

I had one 'crack rock' left when I made it to my friend's house. Her husband flushed it down the toilet and took me to rehab. Rehab didn't work. I thought they would feel sorry for me and give me some money to help get my life back in order. Silly me! When that didn't become my reality, I left the facility…and got high.

Finally, I got sick and tired of being sick and tired. I didn't want my son to live with the legacy that his mother died from crack. It was time to quit once and for all, but I knew I couldn't do it alone. I prayed a simple prayer: *"Help me, God"*—and He did! God delivered me from the demons of drug addiction. I gave it over to God and whenever I even **THOUGHT** of going back, I heard a firm voice say, ***"If you go back, you will surely die"***.

I was finally sober, but also lonely. Loneliness is a dangerous emotion. What did I do in response? I found and married another man. We had been friends, but I wanted to be married. I thought that this time, it would be a Cinderalla marriage. It wasn't, and I left after two weeks.

Living in Atlanta and being drug-free, it was time to get my life back on track. I went to school, got a job, and met another man. Today, he and I are happily married. I **finally** have a man who really loves me.

While volunteering for a nonprofit, I attended a workshop in November 2011. The class was on forgiveness and healing from past hurts. I called my grandfather in the middle of that meeting and told him, *"I forgive you for what you did to me"*. He said, *"Okay. Thank you"*…and hung up! Needless to say, I wasn't expecting him to **admit** it; but I got my healing! That was the beginning of my deliverance from the demons of my youth.

On March 6th, 2012, while I was taking a shower, I saw red hands floating. I asked God, *"What is this?"* He replied, *"Touch me not"*. I asked Him what it is He wanted me to do with all of my experiences. I was directed to start a nonprofit called *Touch Me Not, Inc.*—an organization designed to help women who have been sexually abused as children. Since its inception, many have come through to be saved and set free. God is so **AMAZING**!

Through all the stains put on that apron, all the pains, and all the disappointments, there is still hope once you give it over to God and hold Him to His Word. You are worthy. You were created to have life more abundantly than the stains on the apron.

There is Hope *and* **"LIFE AFTER"** the Apron!

Chapter Seven

There is "Life After..." Waiting for Manifestation

By: Nikki Ruffin

I remember when I first heard about the *Law of Attraction*. It was as if I had discovered the earth, wind, and fire. It was just that fantastic to me. Well, 'fantastic' can't even begin to describe the **fullness** of the way I felt. It was as if the light had been off and then someone clicked "ON"! The thing about it is this: I knew I was in the dark. I knew I was in my own hell. I knew there was something else…something better. I just didn't know how to get it. The great part about my misfortune is that I was trying to find the light, and then the light found me!

I grew up in church. I knew there was a **GOD**. What I was told, though, was that there was this **GOD** outside of me who controlled me and everything else around me. What I found unbelievable was this this **GOD** would be the author of good as well as bad. How? Impossible, I always thought. To me, the image of *MY GOD* was likened to my grandfather. He was kind. He was stern. He was loving. What I discovered—**OR** shall I say "remembered" later—is that the great energy I call 'God' doesn't move and shake just because I or any others want Him to. There are laws that govern this world. Spiritual laws are universal and unchangeable. They are set in stone, just like Law of Gravity is forever and ever. Amen.

Getting reacquainted with what I had forgotten as a physical being was like food to me. I ate it. I slept it. I longed for it. I longed for everything spiritual. Initially, it wasn't easy to totally embrace. As time progressed, I even began to accept the spiritual wisdom as I accepted the wisdom of my grandparents and their parents. I began to have faith. I began to believe that I controlled my destiny. I had to believe this in order to live my life without going mad. I figured if my destiny was in the hands of someone else, I might as well die. I could not live knowing that. That's a scary thought. So, what did I do? I began to test what I had learned. According to the Word of God, I had every right to do so!

"Beloved, believe not every spirit, but try the spirits whether they are of God: because many false prophets are gone out into the world. Hereby know ye the Spirit of God: Every spirit that confesseth that Jesus Christ is come in the flesh is of God: And every spirit that confesseth not that Jesus Christ is come in the flesh is not of God: and this is that spirit of antichrist, whereof ye have heard that it should come; and even now already is it in the world. Ye are of God, little children, and have overcome them: because greater is he that is in you, than he that is in the world. They are of the world: therefore, speak they of the world, and the world heareth them."

1 John 4:1-5 (KJV)

I believed the True Word would not disappoint. I used the techniques I used as a child (without knowing what I was doing at the time). I began to visualize. I started writing down what I desired. I started creating vision boards and holding desires in my mind until I drifted off to sleep. Guess what? One by one, they manifested. Now, don't get me wrong: I won't pretend that every moment and every second was filled with bliss. There were challenges like we face every day. So, remember: We are still living in a physical world as spiritual beings.

Still, I continued…even during some long, dark days. I posted pictures of my husband and me *(I really wanted love)*. I posted pictures of the money I wanted *(all of it was not in my account yet)*. I posted pictures of a jazz band I was signing in. I posted my Master's degree hanging on the wall. I posted a picture of a baby. I posted a house *(representing my home being saved after almost being foreclosed on)*. I posted an apartment that I needed due to my military duty.

One by one—and rather quickly—each item manifested! At one point, I was taking pictures down weekly because of their manifestation. I asked for an apartment, right? The picture of that apartment was a one bedroom. Now, check this out: Never once did I think about whether the apartment would comfortably house my husband, me, our things, and our dogs. **LOL!** Yes, husband appeared and we were tightly loving one another in my one-bedroom apartment. Thank God it takes nine months to birth a baby! We three would have been tightly loving each other in that **one** bedroom. The lesson here is to really think about what you desire because sometimes, it shows up **just** like you asked for it.

When we finally moved, the money came. It was discovered that I had been underpaid for three years. **YES!** That was $50,000.00 minus taxes. We had a ball! We paid off some debt and prepared for the arrival of our baby girl. ***Isn't that something?***

What did I miss? If I missed anything, I'll make it up when I manifest my new desires. Manifestation always leads to a "Life After…"

If you want more details or coaching on what **you** can do, contact me via email at exhaletoexcel@gmail.com.

Chapter Eight

There is "Life After..." Releasing the Illusion of Control

By: Soul Dancer

There is (a good) "Life After" growing up in a dysfunctional family. How about a little backstory?

On Christmas morning (a few days after my 5th birthday), my life took a fundamental turn. Why? Dad died at the ripe old age of 49. He was a father of nine, with three of us still living at home. Twenty-six years later, I learned just how dysfunctional my family was before Dad married my Mom. Shortly after my 32nd birthday, I learned Mom basically hijacked Dad from one of her sisters. It seems dear, old Dad knocked up who would then have to be his wife (back in 'those days', guy who got gals pregnant were honor-bound to marry the mother of their children). Imagine spending **every** holiday with a sister who not only stole your boyfriend, but served as an aunt to nine children! So, before I was even conceived, let alone born, my family was knee-deep in dysfunction. Because I was born and raised into such dysfunction, I frankly had no clue how deeply I adopted and adapted to doubt, guilt, shame, and worry—lock, stock, and barrel!

Google 'dysfunctional family', and you will most likely see:

"A dysfunctional family is a family in which conflict, misbehavior, and often child neglect or abuse on the part of individual

parents occur continually or regularly, leading other members to accommodate such actions. Children sometimes grow up in such families with the understanding that such an arrangement is normal."

Thanks to the support born from familial piety, my elder brothers and sisters (I'm the youngest of the lot; two sisters, two brothers), along with a solid caste of relatives and neighbors, I grew up thinking I was in a normal household living a normal life. Little did I understand what my "normal" was until a week-long visit with my eldest sister ("Sis") some 20 years ago while in my early thirties. During five nights of post-dinner steamy hot tub talks (to tame winter's chill), I learned just how dysfunctional my youth was.

As Sis' insights soaked in like rain on parched ground, all sorts of revelations sprouted! For example, I **finally** understood why Mom was so unpopular with the rest of the family. After all was said and done, Mom poured her heart and soul into big family meals and events. She volunteered every week to teach knitting at the local community center. To me, she seemed stable, kind, dedicated, and loving. Yet, I recall how Mom consistently complained how her children didn't visit as much as she'd like. It was true. Like clockwork, my relatives appeared at respective events such as birthdays and holidays. Equally true was their absence between traditional family events. Outside of family emergencies, I don't recall folks "just dropping by". When family did visit, it seemed they needed to go after their prerequisite attendance was duly noted.

There is Life After...

Two emergencies that rattled the family tree included the times Mom decided life was too difficult to live. Post-suicide attempts guilt-tripped both my sisters as well as my aunts and grandmothers into the role of 'Mother'. Sis was raising a family of three on her own (Sis is 22 years older than I am). My other sister (eight years my senior) became the default babysitter when my brothers were (often) too busy to look after me. After Mom's first suicide attempt, my elders dealt with the fallout as best they could. One way my brothers and sisters likely coped with Mom's maternal demands was to treat me as their child (versus their brother). Accordingly, my childhood relations with my brothers and sisters are far from normal.

Shortly after my 32nd birthday, I decided to grapple with the rapidly-growing disconnect I felt with my biological family. The primary source for this disconnect? At eight years old, I consciously decided to hide who I really was. You may ask, *"How can an eight-year-old make such a decision?"*, right? Frankly, it was **easy**! I got caught "fooling around" with a neighborhood boy / friend. In my heart of hearts, I wanted him to be my boyfriend. When another neighborhood boy tattled on us…I'm sure you can imagine how a devoutly Catholic single mother would act, yes? I was grounded—for one week, and received nightly spankings before going to an early bed. That week, I realized life wasn't going to be easy for a boy who falls in love with other boys.

Based on what streamed from the Sunday morning pulpit (spanning 13 years, that's 676 masses), souls like me were damned to eternal Hell. As a young, gay soul grappling with the reality he lives in a harsh world, I did what most same-sex oriented souls do: I created two different lives. I decided it was an easier 'choice' being ridiculed and beaten because I was a fatso rather than a faggot.

My path to morbid obesity was planned, since most family members died early due to complications attributed to morbid obesity. With every pound gained, less attention was paid to me—unless it was time to 'pick on the fatso'. Within a couple months post 32nd birthday, I faced a Type-2 Diabetes diagnosis. If I didn't course-correct my habits, my fate would mirror that of my elders': dead by sixty. Thinking life was halfway over, something inside me snapped. I sensed there was far more to life than an early death based on a decision to hide behind a growing girth. My inner voice clearly told me how to become healthier by getting to know the roots of my dysfunction: my family. First on the agenda was getting to know my elder sisters and brothers as siblings…**NOT** as drafted babysitters.

I decided to accomplish two tasks when I called upon the souls I knew the least about. *Task one:* Get to **_KNOW_** them as a brother or sister. What was their life like with mom? What life lessons have they learned that I may harvest and savor like ripe apples on the 'tree of life'? *Task two:* Come out—as in directly state the fact that I'm a happy, healthy, gay soul.

I worked to release my any expectations I had for each visit. I came to terms with the reality my first visit may very well be my last.

From these visits, I learned the nature of my family's dysfunctions from different perspectives.

"Life After…" releasing the dysfunction of control

The most prevalent dysfunctional issue I wrestled with after Sis' visit centers on the concept of control; control fueled by Catholic dogma (also known as conditional love shrouded in what is supposedly unconditional love). Conditional love engages the tools of doubt, guilt, shame, and worry. Thanks to Sis for taking a major risk by sharing her side of our familial story, I saw my world completely different. I saw how unbelievably controlling I was. I saw how I used doubt, guilt, shame, and worry to manipulate relationships in ways I felt utterly disgusted with myself. I saw what life could be **AFTER** I released the need to hide who I was. I stopped controlling what others thought about me based on how they felt or feel about me. I realized it is 100% out of my control. When I realized I—*and ONLY I*—have the right to choose what I think and how I feel, the illusion of control fades like steam rising from a hot cup of coffee.

"Life After" growing up in a dysfunctional family offers one of the most profound learning experiences one ever encounters. By exploring each dysfunction through the eyes of those involved in creating the dysfunction provides me with insights on how to release what blocks me from enjoying a hearty, happy, healthy life.

May your exploring **FREE** you to be *YOU*!

Linda H. Williams

Chapter Nine

There is "Life After…" Breaking the Family Chain

By: Ta-Wanda Wilson

I remember when I was young, I used to share a room with my sister and cousin. I used to lay in the bed and say my prayers softly: *"God, please keep my family safe. Don't let my mom die until I am old and have learned everything I need to know from her. I promise I will be good if you just don't take my family away from me."* I used those very same words as I scaredly and silently prayed and cried for my grandmother and everyone else in my family.

At the time, I didn't realize how young and small my family really was. I was around seven years old; my mom around 25. She had my sister at the young age of 16, and I was born when she was 18. Just like many other families, my grandmother was the foundation of the family. Her house was 'the place' everything happened. The white two-story house with a two-car garage and concrete driveway and walkway that led all the way to the back of the house was perfect for rollerskating. There were two peach trees and two pear trees in the backyard that I loved **AND** hated. I loved getting fresh peaches and pears when they were ripe; I hated having to pick up those slimy, rotten fruits with bugs crawling all over them in the summer. Aside from my grandparents' room, there were three other rooms, seven beds, and one bathroom. It seemed to always be just enough room for everyone, whether they were staying or just visiting for a little while.

There were holiday gatherings, summer cookouts, birthday parties, canning, and food cooking going on. Sleepovers were reserved for the grandkids. During the day, my grandmother provided daycare for children in the Social Services system. If you came by after 5:00 p.m., you would find her adult friends there with card games being played, alcoholic drinks being sold, lots of smoking, and blaring music. With all of those things happening at once, not one person who did **not** live there stepped foot in my grandmother's house because the garage had been turned into a multipurpose room. It was **AMAZING** and one of my favorite places to be! The garage-turned-multipurpose-room had cable television, a telephone, a stereo, couches and chairs, and this huge dark wooden bar with barstools. Behind the bar, there were lots of liquor, jars of pig feet and pickled eggs, small bags of chips, shotglasses, a deep freezer, refrigerator, and cash box. My grandparents were the only people in the family who owned their house and cars. Grandmother would also try to teach the grandkids how to have our own candy store by selling snacks to the other kids in the neighborhood.

While still young, I started reading medical journals because I wanted to learn how to read better—and to get out of the "special" reading classes I was in. You see, I could read; just not as fast as everyone else…and don't dare ask me to read aloud! This shy, timid little dark chocolate girl who bites her nails would have died!

My sister was a great student when it came to her work **AND** a very good reader. My favorite cousin who lived with us was also a great student and reader (she and I were the same age). Then, there was me; the girl who was in "special" reading classes, afraid to read in front of the class.

I can remember hoping I could get through the day without the teacher asking me to read aloud. I would pray—with my fingers crossed—that she would not have any of us read aloud, but if she did? ***GOD, PLEASE LET HER START WITH SOMEONE FAR AWAY FROM ME! PLEASE! PLEASE! PLEASE!*** I did this 'thing' where I would count the number of people before me, calculate which paragraphs they would read to determine my paragraph, and then scan for any big words by silently pre-reading my paragraph while sounding out any hard words before my turn came. I couldn't understand why it was easier for me to read and learn the information in those medical encyclopedias, yet struggled with a 5th grade Social Studies book.

Going from elementary to middle school, I remember thinking, *"Finally, I can get away from the embarrassment of leaving class with the "special" readers!"* I was finally leaving it behind. Little did I know: Those classes would follow me to middle school, but now I had to walk in the classroom with even **MORE** people in the hall seeing me go into the "special" class instead of an elective.

All throughout middle and high school, I continued to read the medical encyclopedias. The white and burgundy books grew to be interesting to me. I also found unfamiliar words in the dictionary and used it in a sentence at least three times a day…every day.

Like most kids, we loved listening to "grown folks' conversations". They discussed things like blood pressure pills, water pills, who had what disease, and who died. I started to take notice of a cousin who had a tumor removed, cholesterol issues, diabetes, and lung cancer. My grandmother's health began to fail. At the age of 52, my grandmother passed away after going through cancer protocols and being told she was in remission. The doctors stated there was nothing more they could do. I watched as she laid there asking for help, complaining about the pain. I didn't understand why they couldn't help her. A few months after that devastating diagnosis, she was gone.

I was so angry because she did everything the doctors told her to do, yet she didn't make it to see 53 years old. I started to research the source of my own internal pain. The answer came when I realized the family no longer gathered together like we used to because we all experienced a great loss.

The house was sold, but the memories remained. I remained angry. A short time after that, a great-aunt lost a leg to diabetes and my mother started having some issues of her own going on. By that time, my favorite uncle started showing symptoms associated with diabetes. I told him what he needed to do to fix the issues, but of course, I was "a high school student who didn't know what I was talking about". Needless to say, he didn't listen to me—that was until the doctor told him the same thing. That was my "Ah-Ha!" moment! I looked at what we, as a family, were doing to ourselves: how we ate, what we ate, the lack of exercise, and our poor habits like stressing and staying up late. It was then I saw the lie that was told to my family over and over again. *How do I get my family to listen to me?* I was that child who was not as smart as the others. It was even said that I would probably never go to college. **How do I get them to listen?**

So, what did I do? I saw the lie that said our family's health issues were hereditary! You see, my family was eating **MAYBE** one vegetable a day. We fried foods. We overcooked collards and cabbage, just so they would be soft enough to practically melt in our mouths. We loved sugar, and stress was no stranger to the family.

My senior year of high school, a friend and I decided we were going to stop eating beef. It was an on-again, off-again thing for me (more on than off, but not strict). After going away to college, I started exploring and researching health more and more. I wanted to know everything! About two years later, I decided to become a vegetarian. I also began to realize I was responsible for my day-to-day actions and that the things I do or don't do have a great effect on the outcome of my future. I realized the only way to help my family was to **BE** the change I wanted for my family's health.

As a whole, our family was too young to continue losing family members. I believe my grandmother didn't have to die the way she did if someone had told her to change her lifestyle. Her bad daily habits were the cause of her cancer, high blood pressure, and diabetes. The same applied to my uncle and other family members. We needed to do something different to get a different result.

After changing a lot of things about my own lifestyle, along with becoming a wife and mother, I decided to nurse my children until they were at least 14 – 15 months old. I also chose to **not** vaccinate my children because of the harmful ingredients I knew were in them. I would never serve my children cow's milk because of the hormones they were pumping into them. After all, my children were little humans; not baby calves! I spoke those things to my family with confidence, speaking as a knowledgeable 20-year-old. You can imagine the backlash I received from my family. No one in the family had ever nursed their children. The questions flew at me from all sides.

"So, what; you think your kids are too good to drink formula?"

"Why don't they drink out of bottles?"

"Why can't they have pacifiers?"

"What do you MEAN you are not going to give them medicine unless it is absolutely necessary? All of us had it, and we turned out fine!"

That one statement that hurt me to my heart—and I meant it **HURT**! I found myself crying and questioning myself. *"Was I doing right by my children? They don't come with a handbook or 'how-to-care-for-them' attached. It was all up to me, right?"* Even though that last comment hurt and was said in a joking way, the one that followed pained me even more—but not enough to change my choices. 'They' said, **"You are going to kill your children if you don't let them eat meat and get vaccinated!"**

Have you ever known something and didn't know how you knew it, but you knew it was the right thing to do? That is how I felt. I was okay with bringing my food to the family cookouts and holiday parties (when we decided to go). I was okay with standing up to the doctors who told me the same thing my mother said about 'killing my children', with the difference being this time, I had an arsenal of the latest information on how children were being damaged by vaccines (this was back in 1995). My children fared very well **without** the vaccines and eating all-natural foods. I continued to happily live a natural lifestyle.

Soon, my mother became ill—a very hard pill to swallow because she got her wish to make it past 52 years old (the age her mother passed away). At the age of 54, she died from lung cancer—but not before trying some of the natural remedies I learned about while working in alternative medicine. Mom later decided she wanted to leave this earth on her own terms and in her own way.

After many years of watching me, my sister took notice of what we were doing and decided to change some of her poor habits. Together, our families continue to break the chains of our family's health history. Now, you may read this and think, *"It was only you and your sister's family"*, but for me, I invested in saving my future family as well. You see, my children have harvested the seeds I planted in them. Now ages 19, 23, and 25—non-vaccinated and medication-free—they are a product of RealWellness. They understand the eight essential lifestyle functions and how the body works. If they continue to understand and apply why we do what we do, their conscious minds will continue to shift this world!

Even with my family's dynamics, my mother often stated how proud she was of her children as we matured and came into our own. She would brag to others about our chosen lifestyles and actually became very protective of our choices—but not before she tried to see if my son (at the age of two) would eat a piece of chicken (even at the tender age of two, he chose to not open his mouth to receive it…mom was impressed).

This was the path I had to walk. Walk alone I did—until others caught on and caught up. My health is my everything; my everything is my family. There is **"LIFE AFTER"** the family chains are broken!

Chapter Ten

There is "Life After..." Devastation, Heartbreak, Loss, Depression, and Sadness

By: Toni Dupree

The interesting thing about going through these "Life After" processes is no one can tell you how to do it! Devastation happens on a daily basis, and we all have a front row seat to it; but when it's our devastation, for some reason, we are unprepared.

I thought about this after losing my mother. I had been to numerous funerals, sat by many ailing bedsides, and comforted many who had lost loved-ones. Somehow, none of those experiences helped me. The heartbreak was so severe, I was certain my heart would never mend—and I wasn't even sure I *wanted* it to mend. No matter how comforting people were to me, none healed my broken heart.

People constantly checked on me, invited me to their family dinners, and wanted to come by and visit, but I just couldn't give to anyone nor anything else. I felt incapacitated due to the loss. I describe losing my mother like this:

"Forced to live without something I desperately need."

Depression opened the door for weakness and darkness that blinded me into a lifeless, incapacitated sadness. Losing my mother was the equivalent of me hitting my rock bottom! I could not fathom what in the hell kind of life I could possibly live without her here! I still don't have the answer to that question; I just know I made her very proud when she was here, and I'm committed to doing the same now that she is gone.

After her memorial service, I found myself not being able to catch up with life. I sat down on my sofa in tears and said, *"Lord, whatever you will have me do, I will do it without resistance"*.

Psalm 23 (NIV)

"The Lord is my Shepherd, I lack nothing. He makes me lie down in green pastures, He leads me beside quiet water, He refreshes my soul. He guides me along the right paths for His name's sake. Even though I walk through the darkest valley, I will fear no evil, for You are with me; Your rod and Your staff, they comfort me. You prepare a table before me in the presence of my enemies. You anoint my head with oil; my cup overflows. Surely, Your goodness and love will follow me all the days of my life, and I will dwell in the house of the Lord forever."

After waking up and asking God for the hundredth time, *"Why do you keep waking me? I have nothing to live for now"*. I remember wanting to die every day after my mother's passing. The feeling was so strong, I felt like I could actually will death to come to me…**BUT GOD!** My mother's favorite Psalm was the 23rd Psalm. I woke up one of those depressing, sad mornings, dropped to my knees, and recited the 23rd Psalm aloud. I read this Psalm every day and sometimes at night before falling asleep. I could feel my heart start to mend…the darkness lightened and my sadness began to fade.

I made a point to make one small step each day towards figuring out what my purpose was. This was the beginning of my *"There is Life After…"*

You see, I realized at this moment, my life-altering tragedy was developing me for my purpose. However, I had to first come to terms with understanding that my mother gave me life, not purpose. So, my wanting to die because she died was an unacceptable plan. Still, I needed to know: **"Why?"** I had to answer some other questions, as well as do some personal groundwork. For example, I needed to know why I'm alive, and now that I committed to getting up every day, I had to know why (it couldn't be because of the 23rd Psalm). Knowing why or why not made my choices more than things to do or things to check off my list.

There are some habits I had to acquire in order to make this realistic. I had to live in the moment. Those times when I was sitting alone in thought, my thoughts needed to be about missing my mother. They needed to be about living in her memory. The very heart of a life that is lived purposefully is the idea that all things in life happen for a reason. When we experience hardship, it's here to show us what we're supposed to learn so that we can grow.

I had to focus on one thing. If I was going to live in my mother's memory, then I couldn't be back and forth wallowing in her death. This exists as a natural extension of living in the present moment. There's a lot to be said for being and living in the moment. If we're only focusing on one thing, we won't ever be preoccupied with anything beyond our immediate situation.

When I dropped to my knees while reciting the 23rd Psalm, I needed to make the necessary changes by starting anew the very next morning. Oftentimes, we wait until we have a tangible reason to make a change. By delaying our participation in our personal goals that we've set for ourselves, that means we are essentially delaying our purpose. My mother used to say, *"When it's important enough to do, you'll do it!"*

I made a point to share my gift of service through my business as well as volunteering. After getting out of my dark place, connecting with people seemed to be my life's mission. I took a part-time job with Clinique Cosmetics in an effort to meet different people and get out of my comfort zone. Even though the feelings associated with loss are very painful, it's easy to get used to it. This decision made it possible for me to network and led to many amazing opportunities. Being that I am single and, during this time, lived alone, I worked very hard to not slip back into that dark place.

Every day, we are presented with an opportunity to practice. Practicing our craft every day as a lifestyle rather than 'just a job', we are making a conscious decision to breathe life into it. This could be physical, mental, or spiritual practice—or it could be all of them! The practice defines our lives and what our purpose is for living. We may be many things to many people and have many interests, but we only commit fully on a day-to-day basis to the craft in which we are dedicated. The difference between a life of fulfillment and one of discontentment ultimately comes down to our intention to practice growth every day. We must grow beyond our limitations by our mind, body, or spirit. People who like to talk about living a fulfilled life practice only when it's convenient for them, but people who seek true fulfillment practice when it isn't.

Losing my mother taught me the following:

"God uses individuals who are just minding their own business, living their lives, and just trying to do His will as best they can naturally; not individuals who expect to be used."

I believe that God also has to prepare us for our life's purpose in order to get us to understand:

There is "Life After…"

Linda H. Williams

Conclusion

What does your *"Life After…"* look like? As you have read, the situations that these co-authors faced—although important—more importantly was **how** they handled their lives going forward. That is what shaped their sense of well-being and health.

Just as the cover suggests, there are *"Life After…"* situations throughout our entire lives and beyond. Life is a journey and, as such, we will constantly face transitions in our lives. How have you handled your *"Life Afters…"*? Did you come out better or bitter? Your attitude determines your actions, and your actions determine how you live out your life.

Look at the examples shared in this book. Did you find yourself in any of them? How have you survived? It's important that we evaluate ourselves and face our past to enjoy our present and excel in our future! It's not always that easy. **Believe me: I know.** However, you are not alone in your journey. You are not the first person to have endured a life-altering situation. If you are struggling alone, I encourage you to reach out to someone. Each of the co-authors has provided contact information. If you need someone to share your burden, I encourage you to reach out to them.

Life is not always easy. In fact, sometimes life is downright *hard*; but there is *"Life After…"*! Don't give up. I'm convinced that the majority of people living under bridges are not a product of mental disorders or substance abuse; rather, something happened in their lives that knocked them off-track and they gave up! Giving up is not an option, as you have witnessed these testimonies of not only *surviving* but ***thriving*** in the face of emotional and physical devastation.

God is good and He created us to have life more abundantly! Your abundant life happens after you realize…

There Is Life After…

Meet the Presenter

Linda H. Williams has been homeless, an alcoholic, a victim of domestic violence, hopeless, and helpless. Everyone has a past. Is your future being held hostage by your past? Linda is now an Author, Insight & Wisdom Coach, Facilitator, Motivational Speaker, and Radio Host. She uses her gifts and talents to empower and encourage women to release the chains of their past. Her passion is to influence women in such a way as to inspire them into positive action. Her mission is to get them from where they are to a place where they can love the life they live.

She facilitates several support groups, workshops, seminars, and provides inspirational speaking for many women's causes. She provides life skills to the women's Prison system, Dismas Charities, Inc., a half-way house, and continues to work with community-based programs offered through local agencies. Linda also provides professional development to local colleges and businesses.

Linda is the author of *Your Past Has Passed* and *There Is Life After…* and Host of the "Phenomenally Yours" radio show on BlogTalkRadio.com and WeSpeakLife.com.

Linda has a degree in English and is a Certified Insight & Wisdom Coach.

Connect with Linda H. Williams at:

www.Lindahwilliams.com
www.beginningtodayinc.org
linda@lindahwilliams.com

Meet the Authors
(in order of appearance)

Dr. Brenda T. Bradley has had a remarkable career and life that has taken many twists and turns. From being a US service member in the Air Force to being a Certified Health Coach, the one common denominator has been a desire to serve others and make the world around her a better place to live in.

Her career began in 1986 when she joined the U.S. Air Force. Throughout her military career, she led and supported many phases of supply chain management, across multiple platforms and regions around the world. Her roles while in the Air Force were positions such as logistics support manager, material acquisition manager, and supply chain analyst. She managed and supervised personnel including foreign nationals in two countries.

As a certified health coach and loving mother of two, her goal is to inspire others to lead the charge for healthy eating and exercise. She attended Hallelujah Acres' Health Minister training in Gastonia, North Carolina. She received additional training at the Institute for Integrative Nutrition in New York.

Dr. Bradley leads workshops on nutrition and offers individual health coaching. Her main focus is to help individuals improve their health and lifestyles. She is a bestselling author and has written and released several books: *Kale Yeah It's Good Cookbook*; *I Feel Good*, and *Fitness Shift*.

She received her doctoral degree in Organization & Management from Capella University; her Master of Human Relations from the University of Oklahoma; and her undergraduate studies were completed at Wayland Baptist University.

Connect with Dr. Brenda T. Bradley at:

www.drbtbradley.com
www.instagram.com/docbrad67
www.twitter.com/drbrendabradley

There is Life After...

Lolitha Y. Terry is a single divorced mother of three, an upcoming Author, Inspirational Speaker, Transformation Coach, and Entrepreneur.

Lolitha is an outstanding example of how to beat the odds when they are stacked against you. She has taken being a victim of depression, broken relationships, divorce, single parenting, and financial distress to a trailblazing position of victory. Starting over after the age of 40, Lolitha is gravitating more and more into her God-given purpose of helping women from all walks of life and diverse backgrounds to prosper by preparing them to live their best lives ever. In her upcoming books, *The P 5 Blessings* and *Girl Get Your Power Back*, Lolitha shows all women, regardless of where they are now, how she has been able to heal and move from Pain to Peace, Purpose, Prosperity and Power.

She is using the principles of the Kingdom to soar to levels in life that we only dream about. Lolitha believes "it's not about how you started, but how you finish", and that your past, your occupation, or your education, do not define who you are. Lolitha will show you how to find the blessings of God in every stage of life—even in the Pain! Lolitha's ultimate desire is see women FREE and Prospering.

In her free time, Lolitha loves learning, writing, and speaking. Now, she is endeavoring to travel and see the world. She has always been called, "The life of the Party"—the one who makes everyone laugh. She loves seeing people happy and prospering because at the end of the day, we should! Life has not been without challenges, nor has it been EASY; but she loves the way God has taken all of her pain to fuel her passion.

Connect with Lolitha Y. Terry at:

http://facebook.com/lolithat

There is Life After...

Melissa A. Secka is a native of Cherryville, North Carolina. Mrs. Secka's educational background is in Early Childhood Education. However, it is her own tragic childhood involving incest, child exploitation, and mental abuse—which further fuels her passion to eliminate childhood sexual abuse, as well as educate families and communities.

She is a Certified Life Coach and a Facilitator for Stewards of Children. She has been in the Mental Health field for over 20 years. Her passion and focus are to educate others on how to prevent sexual abuse in the lives of children everywhere. Mrs. Secka and her staff stand ready and willing to assist other organizations and the community at large, in learning how to identify and prevent childhood sexual abuse.

Connect with Melissa A. Secka at:

touchmenotinc@yahoo.com

Nikki Ruffin-Smith

Author, Speaker, Coach & Advocate of STEM/STEAM

Nikki Ruffin-Smith devotes her time as an influencer of change in the education system. She accomplishes this mainly through her writing. Nya Knows Numbers is a product of Nikki's love for educational evolution.

Although Nikki has written several books, her focus is to support the STEM/ STEAM effort by pushing her children's book series. In the first book of five, two year old Nya is showing her love for math by counting, adding, displaying numbers in numerical form, and displaying numbers in written form. Through the entire series, readers are provided a wonderful curriculum which compliments all the books.

Books available on Amazon.com

Contact me at: 205-533-0121
exhaletoexcel@gmail.com

Nikki Ruffin-Smith is a Success Strategies teacher at Nossi Art College and an assistant preschool teacher at Blessed Beginnings CLC. She's a retired Army Officer of 28 years. She's also a married mother of three Residing in Nashville, TN. Nikki has a bachelors in Individualized Studies (Virginia State University); Masters of the Humanities (Tiffin University, Ohio).

There is Life After...

Soul Dancer enjoys a unique birth name, as well as a life as a private Spiritual Teacher, Coach, Keynote Speaker, Live-Talk Radio Show Host, and Syndicated Columnist. Soul is the Founder of Soul University and Author of *Pay Me What I'm Worth*. His life journey includes earning a Master's in Social Work and a Bachelor's in Human Relationships from the University of Minnesota. His travels take him to 20+ countries to receive training and offer teaching as a Social Worker, Monk, and Shaman.

Soul is also a Monk on a mission. Goal: To care for caregivers locally and globally.

Former clients include: Ameriprise, I.B.M Global Services, Wells Fargo, Wells Fargo Home Mortgage, Wells Fargo Trust Operations, The American Red Cross, and The American Association of Blood Banks. His volunteer work (from Board member to the frontlines) include: Outfront Minnesota , Chicago's Center on Halsted, San Diego's The Center, as well as a variety of helplines and pride groups.

Connect with Soul Dancer at:

https://souluniversity.org
https://paymewhatiamworth.com
https://bit.ly/payradio

Linda H. Williams

"Improve your health naturally by shifting your daily lifestyle choices."

Ta-Wanda Wilson is a board-certified Holistic Health Practitioner and Wellness Educator for RealWellness, LLC with over two decades of experience. Ta-Wanda's passion is helping people with chronic lifestyle diseases who want to improve their health, don't like taking medication, or have seen family members with the same issues take the traditional route and they don't want to go down that road.

Ta-Wanda created the 8 Essential Lifestyle Functions as a guide to naturally rebuild, repair, recover, and prevent lifestyle diseases. She has been successful in assisting clients in achieving their optimal health goals by way of coaching, consulting, and workshops for nonprofits, small businesses, and thousands of clients.

Ta-Wanda attended Norfolk State University for undergrad and holds specialties as a Certified Clinical Chiropractic Assistant through Life Chiropractic College West and the North Carolina Board of Examiners, North Carolina Board Certified Radiologist Technologist, and Certified Holistic Nutrition + Wellness Consultant.

There is Life After...

She spent 18 years working in clinical settings alongside give amazing Holistic and Specialty doctors.

This provided the hands-on training that equipped her with extensive knowledge of holistic health, innate healing, wellness consulting, and preventative health. Ta-Wanda continues to further her education, studying a variety of alternative health theories, practical lifestyle management techniques, and innovative coaching methods.

Connect with Ta-Wanda Wilson at:

realwellnesscorp.com
facebook.com/realwellnessllc
instagram.com/realwellness_llc

Toni Dupree is Founder and President of Etiquette & Style by Dupree (ESD), an etiquette training and coaching company based in Houston with a mission to help young people and business professionals get ahead with good manners. Since 2006, her etiquette workshops, style seminars, and self-esteem and behavior classes have taught hundreds of individuals—from youth groups to business gatherings—how to present their best selves and cultivate meaningful, productive relationships.

A Houston native, Toni was introduced to the social graces as a child when she attended Mildred Johnson's Charm and Etiquette Academy. Her training there helped prepare her for work as a Model, Pageant Participant, Speaker and Facilitator. She is a graduate of the Interior Arts School of Design in Houston, Texas and Jack Yates High School. Toni has also earned certification from the Center for Organizational Cultural Competence in Winnipeg, Canada and completed coursework in Psychology and Behavioral Analysis from Kaplan University.

Prior to launching ESD, Toni volunteered as a youth mentor at Houston's Trinity United Methodist Church, organizing self-esteem workshops, fashion show preparation sessions and etiquette classes for young people. While working as a trainer at the Houston Area Women's Center, she developed Business Etiquette workshops and taught Life Skills classes for the organization's clients, laying the foundation for the creation of ESD in 2006.

In addition to offering customized etiquette workshops, business environment training and life skills coaching sessions to young adults and business professionals in Houston and beyond, Toni published her first book in 2015, *Whose Fork is it Anyway*?, an entertaining and easy-to-read dining guide for young adults. Toni lives in the Houston area, where she volunteers with Makeover 101, a non-profit ministry; Village of Winkler, an elderly community; and Houston Can Academy, a second chance high School for teens considering dropping out of high school.

Connect with Toni Dupree at:

832-407-3117
Chytonya.dupree@yahoo.com
www.dupreeacademy.com
Follow us on: Facebook | Instagram | Twitter

Appendix

Dysfunctional family - Wikipedia
https://en.wikipedia.org/wiki/Dysfunctional_family

James, G. (2012). *Turn Failure into Success: 10 Ways. The first step to becoming more successful is changing the way you think about failure.* https://www.inc.com/geoffrey-james/turn-failure-into-success-10-ways.html

www.ingramcontent.com/pod-product-compliance
Lightning Source LLC
Chambersburg PA
CBHW070543300426
44113CB00011B/1780